W9-BEQ-283

In the early 1730's, a group of Englishmen, including General James Edward Oglethorpe, planned to colonize a region to be called Georgia in honor of King George II. Their proposal intended to send imprisoned or released debtors to the settlement. The initial plan failed, but General Oglethorpe obtained a 21-year charter from King George to establish a colony that would allow worthy poor people to immigrate to America and supply Great Britain with silk and wine as well as create a stronghold against imperialistic Spanish Florida.

Although Spain, which had previously claimed the area, protested to England, Oglethorpe and the first band of about 115 settlers sailed from England on November 17, 1732. They arrived on February 12, 1733, at Yamacraw Bluff, the site of present-day Savannah. Tomochichi, a Creek chief whose tribe lived nearby, assisted the colonists and helped persuade other Creek tribes to accept the settlers. Within a few months, Oglethorpe signed a formal treaty with 50 tribes of the Lower Creek Nation. In the 21 years that the Charter Group controlled Georgia, more than 4,000 settlers arrived.

Savannah became one of the first planned cities in America. It was built according to a grid designed by William Bull and Oglethorpe. The plan called for the city to be divided into wards, each composed of 40 house sites. Two lots were set aside on each square for public buildings. The first six wards were laid out by 1736. Construction continued into the next century and by 1856, Savannah had 24 squares. All but three squares survive today.

The earliest colonial houses were built of wood on a foundation of 1-1/2-inch planks raised on logs two feet above the ground. The structures consisted of a large room, two smaller rooms and a loft, within a layout 24 feet long by 16 feet wide. Builders used a form of local stucco called "tabby," mixed of lime and oyster shells, to reinforce walls. Chimneys and foundations were strengthened with bricks and stones sent from England on ships as ballast.

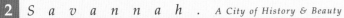

One of the city's favorite places is the esplanade along the waterfront where visitors enjoy strolling, shipwatching, and shopping. The old warehouses, restored from the halcyon days of King Cotton, also feature many fine restaurants and shops. Scenic cruises along the inter-coastal waterway offer additional sightseeing.

The Waving Girl

The Waving Girl is one of Savannah's most endearing symbols. The sculpture is dedicated to Florence Martus, a local resident, who for 44 years, waved a welcome to each incoming ship and a goodbye to every outgoing ship to and from the Savannah Harbor. She died February 8, 1943. The monument by Felix de Weldon was erected in 1971 by the Altrusa Club of Savannah.

THE PORT CITY

Savannah's land-locked port is one of the largest in the southeast and is used by import and export merchants from around the world.

During the period when Savannah ranked first as a cotton seaport on the Atlantic and second in the world, the Cotton Exchange Building was constructed in 1887. The historic structure was designed by Boston architect William Gibbons Preston and was the first building in the United States to be erected directly over a public street. For many years, the Cotton Exchange was the hub of Savannah's economic activity.

Entrances to Bay Street buildings known as "Factor's Row," dating from the days when cotton dominated the economy, are linked to a high bluff by iron bridges. Cobblestone streets were laid from stones that were used as ballast in the holds of trading ships and were dumped ashore when they were no longer needed.

JOHNSON SQUARE

Laid out in 1733, Johnson Square is the first of Savannah's original 24 squares. Prominently located on Bull Street between Bryan and Congress Streets, the square was named for Oglethorpe's friend, Governor Robert Johnson of South Carolina. From the early colonial days, Johnson Square served as the village center where residents gathered to discuss news, post notices, draw water, and meet many important visitors. Famous guests over the years included President Monroe in 1819, the Marquis de Lafayette in 1825, and Daniel Webster in 1848. The public mill and oven were located on this square. The city's first "skyscraper" was erected here in 1911 by the Savannah Bank. Currently, the square is the city's banking center, with many other banks located here. A monument in the center of the square designates the gravesite of General Nathanael Greene, a Revolutionary War hero who died in 1786.

JOHNSON SQUARE

Johnson Square is named for Governor Robert Johnson of South Carolina who befriended the colonists when Georgia was first settled. It was laid out by Oglethorpe and by Colonel William Bull in 1733, and was the first of Savannah's squares. In early colonial days the public stores, the house for strangers, the church, and the public bake oven stood on the trust lots around it.

Events of historical interest are associated with Johnson Square. Here in 1735, Chekilli, head Chief of the Creek Nation, recited the origin myth of the Creeks. In 1737, the Rev. John Wesley, after futile efforts to bring to trial certain indictments against him growing out of his ministry at Savannah, posted a public notice in this Square that he intended to return to England. The Declaration of Independence was read here to an enthusiastic audience, August 10, 1776.

In 1819 a ball was given for President James Monroe in a pavilion erected in the Square. Eminent men who have spoken here include the Marquis de Lafayette, (1825); Henry Clay (1847), and Daniel Webster (1848). Beneath the Nathanael Greene monument rest the remains of the famous Revolutionary general and his son.

Christ Church (Episcopal) was the colony's first house of worship. It was founded in 1733 by Oglethorpe on the east trust lot of Johnson Square. One of its most famous rectors was John Wesley, the third rector, who served in 1736 and 1737. Wesley began a Sunday School program for children that is believed to be the first in the country. Also, he published the first English hymnal in America. Another well-known rector was George Whitefield who served intermittently from 1738 to 1740. Whitefield's preaching raised money for the colony's Orphan House which he named Bethesda.

The present structure replaced previous buildings that had burned or been razed. The impressive building, designed by James Couper and built in 1838, is an excellent example of early Greek Revival architecture in America.

JOHN WESLEY, 1703-1791
Founder of Methodism

On the "trust lot" south of President Street and immediately west of this square stood in 1736-37 the parsonage in which John Wesley resided. In the adjoining garden he read, prayed and meditated. Weekly meetings of members of his Christ Church congregation were held in the small wooden dwelling. According to Wesley, "The first rise of Methodism was in 1729 when four of us met together at Oxford. The second was at Savannah in 1736 when twenty or thirty persons met at my house."

The monument here was dedicated in 1969. Wesley is depicted at the period of his Georgia ministry, wearing his Church of England vestments. The sculptor Marshall Daugherty says of this rendering: "The moment is as he looks up from his Bible toward his congregation, about to speak and stretching out his right hand in love, invitation and exhortation. In contrast, the hand holding the Bible is intense and powerful - the point of contact with the Almighty..."

Located on Abercorn Street between Congress and Bryan Streets, this square was first named Lower New Square and was laid out in 1734. It was renamed for Captain John Reynolds, the first Royal Governor of Georgia in 1754. A public filature warehouse was built on the northeast trust lot and was the center of the silkworm effort that trustees hoped would lead to the establishment of silkworm plantations in the colony.

In 1969, Georgia Methodists erected a monument to their founder, John Wesley, on the site of what they believe to have been his parish home and gardens. The black marble work was created by Marshall Daugherty who depicted Wesley at the age of 33 when he first arrived in Savannah wearing vestments of the Church of England. Wesley first served at Christ Church on Johnson Square in 1736 to 1737 and became a leader in the new Methodist movement in the early 1740's.

Named for the shade of stucco that covers its old bricks, the Olde Pink House was built in 1771 for James Habersham, Jr., a prosperous merchant and public servant. Among other successes, Habersham helped to establish the University of Georgia. The house survived the great Savannah fire of 1796 that destroyed two-thirds of the city, including 300 homes. The house is an excellent example of Georgian architecture. During the War Between the States, the home was taken over by Federal troops and used as headquarters for General York. Today, the historic house is a popular restaurant.

Located on Barnard Street between State and York Streets, this square was originally named St. Jame's Square and was one of the city's most fashionable residential districts. In 1833, the square was renamed to honor Edward Telfair, three-time governor of Georgia, and his family.

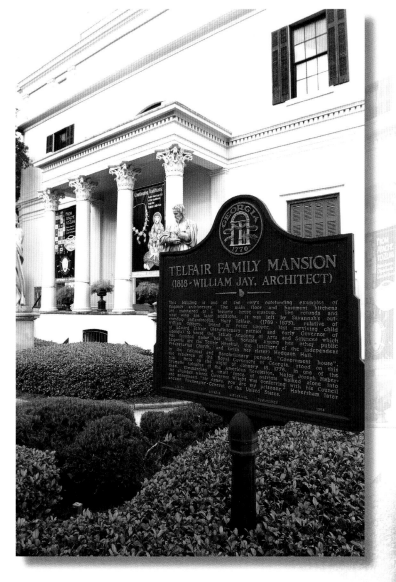

The Telfair family home, a beautiful Regency mansion, was designed by William Jay and completed in 1819 for Governor Edward Telfair's son, Alexander. Mary Telfair, the family heir, bequeathed the house to the Georgia Historical Society in 1875. After a large expansion, the house reopened as the Telfair Academy of Arts and Sciences in 1886, becoming the first art museum in the south. Today, as one of three sites owned by the Telfair Museum of Art, the Academy has on view fine paintings as well as many restored rooms featuring moldings, cornices, original mantelpieces, and other innovations for which Jay is famous.

Telfair's Jepson Center for the Arts

Laid out in 1733 on Bull Street between State and York Streets, this is one of the oldest of the city's squares. Originally named Percival Square, it was renamed to honor Sir James Wright, Georgia's last Royal Governor. It has commonly been called Courthouse Square because from its start, it has held a courthouse on the site. A monument recognizes the contributions of William Washington Gordon, an early Savannah mayor and founder of the Central of Georgia Railroad. In the southeast area of the square, a huge boulder of Georgia granite is dedicated to the memory of Chief Tomochichi, the Creek leader who welcomed Oglethorpe and assisted the colonists.

TOMO-CHI-CHI'S GRAVE

LUTHERAN CHURCH OF THE ASCENSION
(Founded, 1741)

On April 14, 1741, John Martin Bolzius, who as Pastor of the Salzburgers at Ebenezer was in charge of Lutheran work in the colony of Georgia, founded the congregation now known as the Lutheran Church of the Ascension.

In 1756 members of the congregation purchased for one hundred and fifty pounds the lot upon which the present church building stands, directly East of this marker. Around 1772 a nearby building which had formerly served as a court house was acquired at a cost of seventeen pounds and was moved to this site, becoming the first church building of Lutherans in Savannah.

The present church was erected in 1843. Extensive remodeling was completed in 1879 and at that time it was dedicated as "The Evangelical Lutheran Church of the Ascension." The choice of the name is connected with the beautiful stained glass window behind the altar, portraying the Ascension of Christ into heaven.

020-76   GEORGIA HISTORICAL COMMISSION   1960

In 1741, a group of German Lutherans founded the Ascension congregation. Thirty years later, church trustees purchased a lot on the east side of Wright Square and began construction on their permanent sanctuary in 1772. The first frame building burned in 1797 and was rebuilt and used until 1843 when part of the present structure was begun. The completed stone edifice, reflecting Gothic influence, dates between 1875 and 1879. The magnificent Ascension Window was installed in 1879 and the congregation expanded their name to Lutheran Church of the Ascension. While remaining basically the same, the interior has been renovated many times. More art and stained glass windows have been added and the historic church is one of Savannah's main attractions.

JULIETTE GORDON LOW

The birthplace of Juliette Gordon Low, founder of Girl Scouts of the USA, is at the corner of Bull Street and Oglethorpe Avenue. Built 1818-1821 for James Moore Wayne, the mayor of Savannah, a U.S. Congressman, and later a Supreme Court Justice, the house was sold in the 1830's to William Washington Gordon I (Juliette Low's grandfather). Juliette, known as Daisy, was the second of six children. She lived in the Gordon family home until her marriage to William Mackay Low, a wealthy Englishman. While living in England, Daisy met Sir Robert Baden Powell, founder of the Boy Scouts. He introduced her to the Girl Guides. She returned to the United States to start the Girl Guide program in Georgia in 1912. The following year, the name was changed to Girl Scouts. Her program continues as the largest girl serving organization in the world with 3.7 million members.

In 1953, Girl Scouts of the USA purchased the "Birthplace" as it is commonly called by Girl Scouts nationwide. The handsome English Regency house became the city's first National Historic Landmark. The house has been elegantly restored to reflect the Victorian era and is furnished with many original Gordon family pieces, including artwork by Juliette Gordon Low. Now known as the Juliette Gordon Low Girl Scout National Center, the house is open to the public as a museum and to Girl Scouts from around the country as a program center.

On Abercorn Street between State and York Streets, Oglethorpe Square was laid out in 1742. It was originally called the "Upper New Square" but was officially named to honor General James Edward Oglethorpe, the founder of Savannah.

OGLETHORPE SQUARE *cont.*

Owens-Thomas House

On the east side of the square, the historic Owens-Thomas House was built from 1816 to 1819 for Richard Richardson, a cotton merchant, and his wife, Frances Bolton, the sister-in-law of William Jay. Richardson was impressed with Jay, a young, unknown architect, and hired him to design the Richardson's home in Savannah. Jay supervised construction of this magnificent house that many believe is the finest example of English Regency architecture in the United States.

OGLETHORPE SQUARE *cont.*

Owens-Thomas House

A distinctive entrance, with classic Greek details, features curved stairs that lead to the portico, supported by Ionic columns, and into a grand entrance hall. Among Jay's unusual innovations are a brass- inlaid staircase with a unique bridge spanning the central stairwell, a Greek-key-patterned window and amber glass in the dining room, and the artistic drawing room ceiling. The impressive cast iron side porch has four Corinthian columns with elongated floral supports. The house contains many other unique architectural elements, some of which have become known as Jay's trademarks.

OGLETHORPE SQUARE *cont.*
Owens-Thomas House

In 1819, an elaborate plumbing system was installed with rain-fed cisterns, flushing water closets, sinks, bathtubs, and a shower. A rare built-in marble-top table is among the only surviving objects from the Richardsons. Unfortunately, the Richardson family lived in the house only three years before losing it to creditors because of the financial depression of 1820. During the next decade, the house was used as an elegant boarding house. In 1830, George Welshman Owens, congressman, lawyer and one-time mayor of Savannah, purchased the property. The Owens family occupied the house until 1951 when Owens' granddaughter, Margaret Thomas, bequeathed it to the Telfair Academy of Arts and Sciences, now the Telfair Museum of Art. The Owens' family furnishings form the nucleus of the decorative arts collection, which includes outstanding American and European objects dating from 1750 to 1830.

COLUMBIA SQUARE

Laid out in 1799 according to Oglethorpe's plan, Columbia Square, on Habersham Street between State and York Streets, is named for the mythical female figure popularized as a symbol of the new nation in poems during and after the Revolutionary War. The site was the eastern limit of Savannah when the city was walled. Bethesda Gate, one of six city entrances, was located here. In 1970, Wormsloe Fountain was placed in the center of the square as a memorial to the DeRenne family, descendants of Noble Jones, an original colonist who developed Wormsloe Plantation on the nearby Isle of Hope. Today, Wormsloe is a State Historical Site.

Opposite the Wormsloe Fountain stands the Kehoe House that was constructed by iron magnate William Kehoe in 1892 as his family home. The three story Queen Anne structure features cast iron balustrades and railings along the verandas. Kehoe believed that anything that could be made of wood could be made just as well with iron from his foundry.

The elegant Davenport House, located on the northwest corner of Habersham Street, was the catalyst for the founding of Savannah's historic preservation movement. Isaiah Davenport was a master builder who constructed the house as his personal residence in 1820. The home is noted as one of the finest examples of Federal-style architecture in America. Features include overall symmetry, a horseshoe shaped entry stair highlighted with wrought iron ornamentation, a fanlight over the front door, and a solid rectangular shape. It contains fine woodwork, marble mantels, and elegant plaster craftsmanship, as well as early 19th century furnishings. The house was saved from demolition in 1955 by seven Savannah ladies who founded the Historic Savannah Foundation. Over the years, the Foundation has been successful in saving hundreds of buildings through its preservation programs. In 2005, Davenport House received the Preserve America Presidential Award for its accurate restoration and community support.

ORLEANS SQUARE

On Barnard Street between Perry and Hull Streets, this square was laid out in 1815 and named to honor the heroes of the Battle of New Orleans during the War of 1812. In the later 1980's, the German Societies placed a fountain and benches in the square to honor the contributions of early German settlers.

Located on Bull Street between Hull and Perry Streets, Chippewa Square was laid out in 1815 and named for the Battle of Chippewa during the War of 1812. This square was the center of night life in the city during the time that William Jay's lavish Savannah Theatre, completed in 1818, stood on the northwest corner as a reflection of the local prosperity and culture. At the center of the square is James Edward Oglethorpe's monument.

JAMES EDWARD OGLETHORPE
(1696 - 1785)

James Edward Oglethorpe (1696 to 1785) is the founder of the Georgia Colony. One of America's best sculptors, Daniel Chester French, (also known for the Lincoln Memorial in Washington, D.C.) completed the nine-foot bronze statue in 1910. The figure is depicted in full dress of a British general of the period. It faces south symbolizing the threat of Spain's imperial ambitions to the colony. The pedestal and base of the monument were designed by French's associate, Henry Bacon. The four lions at the corners of the base hold shields that depict the coat of arms of Oglethorpe, and the great seals of the Colony of Georgia, the State, and the City of Savannah.

MADISON SQUARE

MADISON SQUARE

Madison Square was laid out in 1839 and is named for the fourth president of the United States. Around the Square stand notable examples of the Greek revival, Gothic, and Romanesque architecture characteristic of nineteenth century Savannah.

To the west are St. John's Church (Episcopal), 1853, and the Green-Meldrim mansion, 1861, (Gen. W. T. Sherman's headquarters). To the north is the Francis Sorrel residence, 1840, which was visited by Gen. Robert E. Lee in 1862 when he commanded the Confederate coast defenses in this area. To the east is the Jewett house, erected 1842. The DeSoto Hotel and the Savannah Volunteer Guards' Armory, of a later period, are in the Romanesque style typical of their designer, William G. Preston, of Boston.

The central bronze monument commemorates the heroism of Sergeant William Jasper (2nd Continental Regt. of South Carolina) who was mortally wounded October 9, 1779, a short distance northwest of this marker, in the unsuccessful assault by the American and French forces upon the British lines, which ran immediately to the north of this Square.

025-71   GEORGIA HISTORICAL COMMISSION.   1959

Located on Bull Street between Harris and Charlton Streets, Madison Square dates from 1839 and was named for James Madison, the fourth President of the United States. In the center of the square is a statue memorializing Sergeant William Jasper who was mortally wounded in the same battle as General Pulaski during the Seige of Savannah.

Located at 1 West Macon Street, this historic home was built in 1853 for a wealthy cotton merchant and ship owner, Charles Green. The style is an exceptional example of Gothic Revival architecture. In 1892, Green sold the house to Judge Peter Meldrim, a former mayor of Savannah. It remained in Meldrim's family until 1943, when it was sold to St. John's Church and restored as their parish house.

The house was used by General Sherman as his headquarters during the occupation of Savannah. Sherman spared the city from his fiery wrath because of its beauty and charm. In the bedroom of the house, the general wrote his famous telegram to President Lincoln: "I beg to present you a Christmas gift, the City of Savannah." It was also from this house that Sherman issued his Field Order #15 granting "40 acres and a mule" to newly-freed black citizens.

SHERMAN'S HEADQUARTERS
Green-Meldrim Mansion

LAFAYETTE SQUARE

This square, located on Abercorn Street between Charlton and Harris Streets, was laid out in 1837. It was named for the Marquis de Lafayette who visited Savannah in 1825 and spoke to crowds of admirers from the balcony of the Owens-Thomas House (Oglethorpe Square) where he stayed as a guest of the city. Until 1846, the city jail was located here; but when it was moved, Andrew Low purchased some of the land to build his residence.

Originally built in the 1870's, the Cathedral of St. John the Baptist was destroyed by fire 22 years later, then completely rebuilt from the original design. The majesty of the stained glass windows and murals complete the splendor and beauty of the Cathedral. It is one of the oldest Roman Catholic parishes in Georgia.

Completed in 1849 for Andrew Low, an English cotton factor and one of the wealthiest men in Savannah, this gracious mansion features balconies with some of the city's most impressive ironwork. Designed by John Norris, one of Savannah's famous trio of architects (including William Jay and Charles Cluskey), the house welcomed many famous visitors, including William Thackeray and Robert E. Lee. Low's son,

William Mackay Low, owned the residence when he married Juliette Gordon in 1886. After William died in 1905, Juliette Low dedicated herself to founding the Girl Scouts in 1912.

The early Girl Scouts met on the property in the carriage house. Mrs. Low lived here off and on until her death in 1927.

Dating from 1851, Troup Square, on Habersham Street between Harris and Charlton Streets, was named for George Michael Troup. He was a congressional representative, governor, senator, and one of only two individuals so honored during his lifetime.

East from Troup Square are two rows of restored houses, part of a pilot program of urban renewal for historic preservation. Eight stucco units, at 410 to 424 East Charlton Street, have distinctive Victorian bay windows, and were built in 1882 by John McDonough of the McDonough and Ballantyne Iron Firm.

At 410 to 424 East Macon Street, the four brick units nearest Troup Square were built in 1885 by Edward Kennedy. John McDonough constructed the eastern four units in 1872.

MONTEREY SQUARE

On Bull Street between Taylor and Gordon Streets, Monterey Square was named to commemorate the capture of Monterey, Mexico, by General Zachary Taylor's military troops. All the buildings on the square, except the United Way building, are original to the site. The 55-foot-tall marble monument in the center of the square is dedicated to the memory of General Count Casimir Pulaski, a brave Polish nobleman who was recruited in Paris by Benjamin Franklin, and joined with the Americans in the Revolutionary War. He was mortally wounded in 1779 at the Siege of Savannah.

The Congregation Mickve Israel Synagogue was founded by 42 Jewish settlers, who arrived at Georgia's colony in 1733, to seek freedom in the New World. The Torah Scroll was brought to Savannah with the colonists. Other cherished possessions of the congregation, including letters from Presidents George Washington, Thomas Jefferson, and James Madison, are displayed in the temple's archives. The present Synagogue, a striking Gothic structure, was consecrated in 1878.

CALHOUN SQUARE

Dating from 1851, Calhoun Square was one of the last to be laid out. It is located on Abercorn Street between Taylor and Gordon Streets and was named for John C. Calhoun, one of the south's greatest statesmen. Calhoun served his country as secretary of state, secretary of war, and as vice president under Presidents John Quincy Adams and Andrew Jackson.

CALHOUN SQUARE *cont.*

Wesley Monumental United Methodist Church

Wesley Monumental United Methodist Church was organized in 1868. The congregation first met in the Chatham Academy then began building a new structure on property that Trinity Church had purchased on Calhoun Square at the corner of Drayton and Gordon Streets. Originally called City Mission and Second Methodist Church, the congregation adopted the name Wesley Monumental Methodist Episcopal Church South in 1875. The structure was not finished for many years. The design has a Gothic Revival influence and is considered one of the most beautiful Methodist churches in America. The spires measure 136 feet and 196 feet in height. The sanctuary seats more than 800 persons. The magnificent Wesley Window opposite the pulpit contains the busts of John and Charles Wesley, who preached to early Savannah as Anglican ministers before the Methodist Church was established. Many other windows are dedicated to Methodism's historic figures.

GASTON STREET

The colorful Gaston Street homes were built during the 1850's and have unusually deep lots and small front yards. Beautiful landscaping and decorative wrought iron entry railings contribute to the popularity of this historic restored area. Many of the homes have been renovated for use as charming hotels and bed-and-breakfast inns.

The stately old homes and ornate iron-work make Jones Street a favorite with visitors.

FORSYTH PARK

Forsyth Park is the largest park in Savannah and is busy with residents and tourists enjoying a myriad of daily activities. The 30-acre park was laid out in 1851 and named for Governor John Forsyth. The park has long been the scene of many Civil War re-enactments and is home to several monuments built to honor historical figures. In addition to the famous fountain in the center, there is the Fragrant Garden for the Blind, an innovative project planted by Savannah garden clubs. A monument to the Confederacy, erected in 1875, presides over Forsyth Park extension, originally the militia parade ground. Within the iron-railed enclosure surrounding the monument are busts of two Confederate heroes: General Lafayette McLaws and Brigadier General Francis S. Bartow. There is also a monument to the Spanish-American War and dummy forts used for training during World War I.

The centerpiece of the main promenade is a beautiful cast-iron white fountain, erected in 1858. The ornate two-tiered fountain has appeared in several movies that were filmed in Savannah, including "Forest Gump" and "Midnight in the Garden of Good and Evil."

Surrounding Forsyth Park are many beatiful Historic Homes including the Chesnutt House. It features colorful clusters of purple wisteria that drape under twin coppered-roof porches.

OLD FORT JACKSON

Authorized by President Thomas Jefferson, Fort Jackson was built in 1808 to protect Savannah from naval attack. Fort Jackson was named for James Jackson (Revolutionary War hero). It is the oldest remaining brickwork fort in Georgia. It was reborn from a Revolutionary War battery and was garrisoned during the War of 1812.

It was enlarged and strengthened between 1845 and 1860 and was occupied by Confederate troops during the War Between the States and served as headquarters for the Confederate River Defenses. By 1864, Union troops occupied the fort. The fort now serves as a National Historic Landmark.

Fort Pulaski was constructed between 1829 and 1847 on Cockspur Island, 15 miles east of Savannah, to guard the sea approach to the city. It was named for General Casimir Pulaski, the Polish war hero who was mortally wounded at the Siege of Savannah in 1779. Occupied by Confederate troops during the Civil War, the fort fell to Union forces in April 1862, following 30 hours of bombardment with rifled cannons. The Union victory marked the first effective use of the rifled cannon against a masonry fortification and because of its success, this battle ended the era of great brick citadels. Fort Pulaski was abandoned in 1885. It has been restored and is a National Park Monument.

TYBEE ISLAND

A lighthouse on Tybee Island was one of the first public structures in Georgia. The original completed in 1736, was constructed with cedar piles and brickwork. Tybee Lighthouse is one of the earliest in American history. The present lighthouse is 154 feet tall (the bottom 60 ft. date from 1773, the upper 94 ft. from 1867) and continues to serve as a welcoming beacon to ships from around the world that arrive daily at the busy port of Savannah.

HISTORIC
TYBEE ISLAND
LIGHT STATION

OPERATED BY THE TYBEE ISLAND
HISTORICAL SOCIETY

HISTORIC OPTIC MAINTAINED
TIVE AID TO NAVIGATION
STATES COAST

VICTORY DRIVE

Victory Drive is considered one of the most beautiful streets in Savannah. Lined with stately trees and grand historical mansions, Victory Drive leads to neighboring Tybee Island.